CCJC

9-03

D1238889

PRESENTED TO
TULSA CITY-COUNTY LIBRARY
BY

Chicago

Lynnette R. Brent

Heinemann Library
Chicago, Illinois

© 2003 Reed Educational & Professional Publishing
Published by Heinemann Library, an imprint of Reed
Educational & Professional Publishing,
100 N. LaSalle, Suite 300
Chicago, IL 60602

Customer Service 888-454-2279

Visit our website at www.heinemannlibrary.com

All rights reserved. No part of this publication may
be reproduced or transmitted in any form or by
any means, electronic or mechanical, including
photocopying, recording, taping, or any information
storage and retrieval system, without permission in
writing from the publisher.

Designed by Herman Adler Design
Editorial Development by Morrison BookWorks
Printed and bound in the United States by Lake Book
Manufacturing, Inc.

07 06 05 04 03
10 9 8 7 6 5 4 3 2 1

Library of Congress Cataloging-in-Publication Data
Brent, Lynnette R., 1965-
        Chicago / Lynnette R. Brent.
            p. cm.
Summary: Introduces the history, geography, resources,
government, and culture of the city of Chicago.
Includes bibliographical references and index.
        ISBN 1-40340-013-X (HC)
        ISBN 1-40340-703-7 (PB)
    1. Chicago (Ill.)--Juvenile literature. [1. Chicago
(Ill.)] I. Title.
        F548.33 .B74 2002
        977.3'11--dc21
                                        2002004555

Acknowledgments
The author and publishers are grateful to the following
for permission to reproduce copyright material:

Cover photograhs by Robert Lifson/Heinemann Library
(top left, top center right); Stock Montage, Inc. (top
center left); Kelly-Mooney Photography/Corbis (top
right); Corbis (bottom)

Acknowledgments
The author and publishers are grateful to the following
for permission to reproduce copyright material:

p.19 Dean Battaglia; pp. 9 (P&S-1914.0001), 12
(Alexander Hesler/ICHi-05726, 14B.L. (ICHi-02792),
15B.R. (ICHi-35037), 16 (ICHi-02845), 17T.R. (ICHi-
10864), 18C (ICHi-17002), 20T and 27B.L. (ICHi-
06185), 20B (ICHi-35038), 21B.L. Chicago Historical
Society; pp. 23T.R., 28B.L. Bettmann/Corbis;
p. 25T.R. Jacques M. Chenet/Corbis; pp. 3B.R.,
25B Sandy Felsenthal/Corbis; p. 28 C.R. Shelley
Gazin/Corbis; p. 18B Robert Holmes/Corbis;
p. 24B.R. Kelly-Mooney Photography/Corbis;
p. 23B Charles E. Rotkin/Corbis; pp. 23C.R., 28T.L.
Underwood & Underwood/Corbis; p. 24B.L. Robert
Lifson; pp. 1, 22, 27B.C., 27B.R. Corbis; pp. 3B.C.,
8B.R., 14B.R., 21B.R. Robert Lifson/Heinemann
Library; p. 6 North Wind Picture Archives; p. 4B Tom
Neiman/Stock Montage, Inc.; pp. 3 B.L., 7, 8B.L., 11,
15T, 17C.R.,18T, 26B.L., 26B.C., 26B.R., 27B. farL.
Stock Montage, Inc.

Special thanks to Eileen Stahulak, Elementary/Primary
Social Science Curriculum Lead, Department of
Curriculum, Chicago Public Schools for her review
of this book.

Every effort has been made to contact copyright
holders of any material reproduced in this book. Any
omissions will be rectified in subsequent printings if
notice is given to the publisher.

Some words are shown in bold, **like this.** You can find
out what they mean by looking in the glossary.

Contents

J 977.3 B75c 2003
Brent, Lynnette R., 1965-
Chicago

Introducing... Chicago!

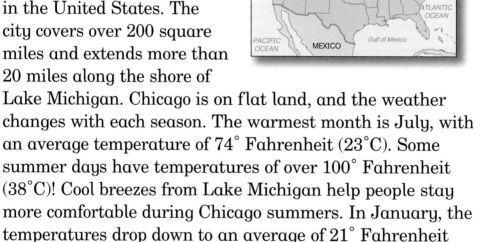

Chicago, Illinois, is located in the Midwest, and is the third largest city in the United States. The city covers over 200 square miles and extends more than 20 miles along the shore of Lake Michigan. Chicago is on flat land, and the weather changes with each season. The warmest month is July, with an average temperature of 74° Fahrenheit (23°C). Some summer days have temperatures of over 100° Fahrenheit (38°C)! Cool breezes from Lake Michigan help people stay more comfortable during Chicago summers. In January, the temperatures drop down to an average of 21° Fahrenheit (-6°C). Very cold days, on which the temperature drops below 0° Fahrenheit (-18°C), are not uncommon!

Many different goods are made in Chicago. In Chicago, you will find iron and steel factories, meatpacking plants, and chemical companies. You will find a huge printing and publishing center. One of Chicago's newspapers, the *Chicago*

Tribune, is read all over the United States. You will notice expressways **sprawling** out in every direction from Chicago, and you will see major ports and railway centers. Downtown Chicago is called "the Loop." Do you know why? Chicago has a system of elevated trains that loop around downtown in a huge rectangle.

What's in a name?

When Chicago became a town in 1833, it covered three-eighths of a square mile. Three hundred fifty people lived there. The name "Chicago" comes from a Native American word, *Checagou,* which many believe means "wild onion." When many Native Americans lived where Chicago now stands, wild onions grew on the rich, **fertile** land.

Some people believe that the word *checagou* had other meanings besides "wild onion." One Native American tribe used the word to describe the Mississippi River and the sound of thunder. So *checagou* might also mean "strong" or "great." As you will see, Chicago is a strong and great city!

Chicago's Flag

Each part of the flag stands for something important about Chicago.

* The three white stripes represent the North, West, and South Sides of Chicago.

* The two blue stripes stand for the two branches of the Chicago River.

* The first star stands for Fort Dearborn.

* The second star stands for the Chicago Fire.

* The third star stands for the World's Columbian Exposition of 1893.

* The fourth star stands for the Century of Progress, an exposition that took place in 1933.

You will read more about these events in later chapters!

Chapter 1

Chicago's Early Days

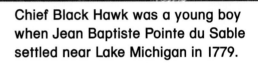

The ground in the area that is now Chicago was often muddy and wet. Winters in the area could be long and very cold. What made this place a good place to settle? The land was **fertile,** so crops could grow. Many animals roamed the land, and rivers flowed through the area. The land is between the Mississippi River and the Great Lakes, so Native Americans had travel routes from Lake Michigan to the Mississippi River. They could travel on land or on the smaller rivers.

Chief Black Hawk was a young boy when Jean Baptiste Pointe du Sable settled near Lake Michigan in 1779.

Native Americans and Chicago

The Illinois Indians were a group of Algonquin Indian tribes. These people were hunters and farmers. They moved around the area and set up camp where they found more animals to hunt and land to farm. They were friendly to the French and English explorers who came through the area.

The Potawatomi Indians came to the Chicago area from Michigan and Wisconsin. Originally they were a hunting tribe. When they moved into Illinois, the women learned farming from other area tribes. Soon, the Potawatomi were growing beans, corn, squash, and herbs that could be used for medicine. Many other Indian tribes also lived in this area with its many animals and rich land.

Exploring Chicago

England and France wanted to claim land of their own in North America, so they sent people to explore this area of the world. In 1673, Father Jacques Marquette and Louis Joliet were sent by the French government to travel on the Great Lakes and into Illinois. They quickly discovered that they could get to the Mississippi River by traveling on smaller rivers in the Chicago area. French fur traders began to use this route to get furs and other goods to ships sailing back to France. More explorers soon followed, setting up camps throughout the area.

When did the Chicago area change from a wilderness area into a settlement? In 1779, one man decided to finally settle and build a home in the area. Jean Baptiste Pointe du Sable came to North America from Haiti. He built a home near Lake Michigan and the mouth of the Chicago River. He married a Native American woman, and their home became an important part of Chicago's history.

Father Jacques Marquette and Louis Joliet were some of the first Europeans to travel through the southern tip of Lake Michigan and the Chicago River.

Fort Dearborn

After the colonists fought and won the **American Revolution** (1775–1783), the U.S. troops fought many Native American tribes in the Midwest. In 1795, the United States government and many tribes signed a peace treaty. As part of the treaty, the Native American tribes agreed to give up land at the mouth of the Chicago River at Lake Michigan.

A few years later, the government built Fort Dearborn. The soldiers in Fort Dearborn protected traders and settlers. Traders and Native Americans often came to the fort to trade furs and other supplies. A few farmers and traders lived on the land just outside the fort.

Why did Native Americans leave Chicago?

The soldiers at Fort Dearborn and the Native Americans living near the fort did not always get along with each other. The trading post at Fort Dearborn brought more and more traders back to the area. Many soldiers who lived in the fort set up farms and other small shops nearby.

The farmers were working the land that the Native Americans depended on for shelter and food. Fur traders were killing the animals that the Native Americans hunted. Slowly, the tribes were being forced out of the area.

Look for Yourself

Fort Dearborn
Today, you can see where Fort Dearborn once stood when you visit the corner of Michigan Avenue and Wacker Drive.

Fort Dearborn was built at the mouth of the Chicago River.

Today, this plaque marks the spot where Fort Dearborn once stood.

In the 1790s, people thought peace treaties would make all people living in the Midwest happy. As time passed, however, the Native Americans were forced to move away.

The government offered each tribe supplies and $5,000 each year in exchange for taking over the land. When the tribes came to the fort each year to get their money, traders and merchants set up a "fair," where people could buy things. The traders made lots of money from the Native Americans, and the Native Americans often went home with a lot of goods that should have cost less than they paid. The Native Americans and the settlers never really agreed on how the land should be used. Eventually, the last of the tribes still living near the fort were forced to live on a reservation far to the west. The Native American tribes who first lived in this area would not be welcomed in the new city named Chicago.

Chapter 2

Chicago Works

Compared to other cities in the early 1800s, Chicago did not have a good location. People could only trade by boat on Lake Michigan or the small rivers flowing nearby. Sailing through the other Great Lakes was difficult. Chicago's settlers wanted to be able to trade and sell goods farther away from Chicago.

Ships and trains come to Chicago

What changed Chicago's ability to **compete?** Railroads and **canals.** Canals were waterways built to connect the Great Lakes so ships could travel from one lake to another. Trees, furs, livestock, and crops could be traded with people who lived northeast of the area. Farmers needed a way to get their crops to Chicago faster. The railroad gave the farmers a fast route to the ships that sailed the Great Lakes.

Chicago becomes an industrialized city

Farmers wanted new farm machines to help them grow and sell more crops. Cyrus H. McCormick came to Chicago and built a machine called the reaper, which helped the farmers gather crops faster.

Trains like this one helped Chicago businesses move goods from place to place.

His factory grew, and thousands of people worked for him. His machines helped the farmers earn more money. They used their money to buy goods from other Chicago **merchants,** so those merchants made more money, too.

All the different **industries** became connected to each other. Businessmen needed factories to keep up with orders. The factory workers needed homes. This helped the lumber industry grow. Many of the new machines were made of steel, so the steel industry grew. Chicago was a leader in the **Industrial Revolution** in the United States.

The stockyards

For many years, cattle were brought to Chicago for food. Cities like Cincinnati were able to ship cattle east because they were on rivers. The **Civil War** (1861–1865), however, brought much of the river traffic to a stop. Many workers came to Chicago to get away from the fighting.

Meatpacking became a big business in Chicago. Meatpacking means getting meat from animals ready for people to eat. At first, the yards that kept the animals were very crowded. Then, the people of Chicago came up with a plan: they would build a new stockyard, a place for the animals to live, with the help of the railroads. On Christmas Day, 1865, the Union Stock Yard opened just south of Chicago. It could hold over 100,000

Chicago became known around the country for its crowded stockyards.

animals, and it was surrounded by train tracks. This made shipping in and out very easy. Once the refrigerated train car was invented, Chicago meats could be shipped as far as the trains would go.

How railroads changed Chicago

The growth of railroads through the Chicago area gave businesses a way to grow. Goods could be bought and sold from across the United States. People who didn't have a skill or weren't able to read could sometimes get jobs with the railroad or the factories.

The railroad also brought new problems to Chicago. The trains and factories made the city very dirty. The houses for the workers were poorly built and crowded. Factory and rail workers were often hurt on the job. These workers were badly needed, but very poorly paid. The city of Chicago was getting richer, but many of its people were suffering.

Immigrants from Europe

People who lived on the East Coast knew that Chicago's factories and railroads were growing. **Immigrants** came to the United States from other countries looking for jobs in Boston and New York City. They heard about new jobs in Chicago. It was not difficult to travel to Chicago from the East Coast. For these reasons, people from all over the world came to Chicago to live.

In the late 1800s, Chicago homes were built close together. This allowed fires to spread easily. Also, there were very few fire departments to fight the fires.

Many Irish Catholics found work on the Illinois Central Railroad. They settled in homes to the south of Chicago, close to their jobs. Many African Americans also moved to the area in the late 1800s when they took jobs in area businesses and as servants in homes.

Germans, Russians, Italians, Greeks, and many other immigrants settled in Chicago. Some opened businesses throughout the city. Unfortunately, some people experienced **prejudice** and could not get jobs and homes.

In the 1880s, immigrant families like this one came to Chicago to start new lives.

A growing danger

When Chicago became a town in 1833, only 350 people lived there. Thirty years later, nearly 300,000 called Chicago home. By 1869, Chicago had over 1,100 factories. Grain storage, the stockyards, department stores, schools, grocery stores, ten railroads, and many more shops had been built. Often, homes and factories were built nearly side-by-side. Mansions for the rich were next-door neighbors to apartment buildings or even shacks. The city government hadn't grown as fast as the city. The city had worked hard on building factories and businesses. Some of the city's needs were not being met.

Some neighborhoods had volunteer fire departments. Many of the fire departments had equipment that did not work very well. The police department didn't have enough officers. No one in the city picked up garbage. Instead, hogs and other animals roamed the streets. They ate the garbage they wanted and left the rest behind. The city didn't provide water to homes. **Sewage** was dumped right into the Chicago River. The city was home to many people and their jobs, but Chicago was one disaster away from being destroyed.

Chapter 3

The Great Chicago Fire

In 1871, most houses in Chicago were built from wood. Even sidewalks and roads were made of wood. In dry months, these structures often caught fire. People would then rebuild the parts that had been burned. The summer and fall of 1871 were drier than usual. Fires were starting all over the city in the beginning of October. Firefighters were exhausted from chasing fires all over Chicago.

The Chicago Fire starts!

On Sunday, October 8, 1871, just after nine o'clock in the evening, a fire broke out in a barn owned by Patrick and Catherine O'Leary. The legend says that the O'Leary cow kicked over a lantern that started the fire. Whether started by the cow or something else, the fire was a **tragedy** for Chicago.

Look for Yourself

The Water Tower
Built in 1869, the Water Tower was a pumping station for Chicago's water supply. It is one of the only buildings in downtown Chicago that survived the Chicago Fire. Today this Chicago landmark is used as a tourist information center. It stands as a memorial to the victims of the Chicago Fire. It is a symbol of Chicago's "I Will" spirit.

The Water Tower was still standing after the fire of 1871.

The Water Tower serves as a tourist attraction today.

While firefighters tried to stop the fire, many people chose to escape the flames by jumping into Lake Michigan. Some even drowned.

The fire destroys Chicago

A strong wind kicked up, and the blaze quickly spread east and north. It leapt across rooftops and down streets. The firefighters could not stop the fire. After two days, rain began to fall. On the morning of October 10, 1871, the fire finally died out. The center of Chicago was completely destroyed. At least 300 people were dead, nearly 100,000 people were homeless, and about $200 million in property was destroyed. The Chicago Fire became one of the worst disasters of the 1800s. Chicago was changed forever. What could the people of Chicago do next?

Firefighters throughout Chicago were called to fight the fire.

Rebuilding begins

The Great Chicago Fire destroyed three and a half square miles of the city. Streets, businesses, transportation, and 100,000 homes were lost in the fire. People around the country believed that Chicago would never recover. But the people of Chicago were determined to rebuild. Within just a few days, some businesses reopened, using shacks as offices. Citizens worked together to rebuild homes and to help homeless people. The city went to work repairing the damage.

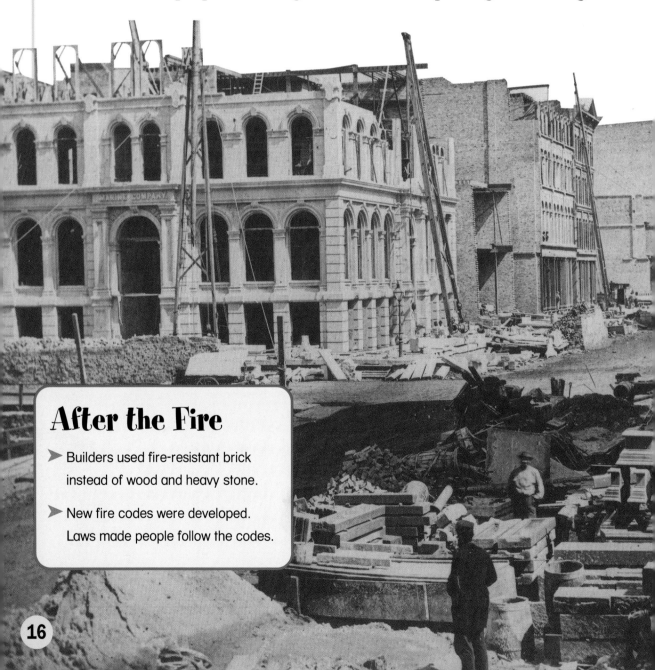

After the Fire

➤ Builders used fire-resistant brick instead of wood and heavy stone.

➤ New fire codes were developed. Laws made people follow the codes.

The new look of Chicago

Architects, people who make designs for buildings, were asked to come help rebuild Chicago. They came to Chicago from around the country to make plans for new buildings. New, modern-looking buildings were soon built where only rubble and ashes were before. Builders began to use concrete and steel instead of wood.

Buildings made of these materials could be built taller, and they wouldn't burn as easily as wooden ones. With incredible energy and **determination,** the people of Chicago built a city even greater than they had before.

Immigrants help Chicago grow

Once rebuilding started, Chicago was again attractive to **immigrants.** Many businesses were looking for workers. Construction companies needed laborers to help them rebuild the burned buildings and create new ones. People came from all over Europe to live in Chicago. These many cultures helped make Chicago a great city.

Chicago People

William Le Baron Jenney
City planners and architects came up with ideas to organize Chicago. William Le Baron Jenney helped design Chicago's new streets in a grid system.

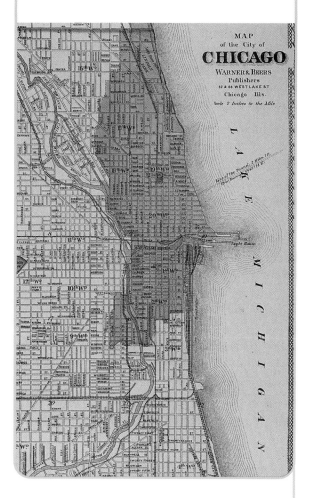

MAP
of the City of
CHICAGO
WARNER & BEERS
Publishers
67 & 64 WESTLAKE ST
Chicago Ills.
Scale 2 Inches to the Mile

Immigrants from around the world sold goods at the Water Street Market on the near Southwest Side at Morgan and 15th Streets.

The trains brought **immigrants** to Chicago. The trains also provided many of the immigrants with jobs. Most of these families wanted to live close to their work and near people with the same culture. Irish Catholic workers settled on the South Side of town. Many German Jews moved to the South Side after losing their homes in the fire. The South Side also became home to a large African-American population. The West Side of Chicago was home to many people from Italy, Poland, Greece, and other parts of Europe.

Look for Yourself

Chicago Parks

City planners believed Chicago should save some areas for large, green parks. Garfield Park was planned especially for workers, including the many immigrants, so many could enjoy their time off. Today, the city is home to more than 500 parks. These parks provide places for people to play, relax, and enjoy city sites. The Chicago Park District offers day camps, nature hikes, sports clubs, and many other exciting activities to Chicagoans.

Garfield Park was built on the West Side of Chicago in the late 1800s.

Today, people can still enjoy the Garfield Park Conservatory year-round.

What did immigrants bring to Chicago?

As the immigrant neighborhoods grew, people started businesses like ones back home. Some people started newspapers, schools, and churches to share their cultures. Others opened restaurants, butcher shops, and bakeries. Many small museums helped to preserve the traditions of the many ethnic groups. In these ways, people helped keep their own cultures alive in their new city. All Chicagoans had the chance to learn about the cultures of their neighbors.

Many of the immigrants' traditions are still celebrated today. The Irish community in Chicago celebrates St. Patrick's Day by holding a huge parade and dyeing the Chicago River green. On certain Greek holidays, Chicagoans with Greek roots perform traditional dances for audiences all over town. German Americans have a huge festival to celebrate with music, food, and dance each May. Churches, schools, cultural groups, and the City of Chicago all sponsor events to celebrate the many cultures of people living in Chicago today.

Today, dancers in Chicago's St. Patrick's Day parade dance like Irish immigrants danced a hundred years ago.

Chapter 4

A Century of Progress

The World's Columbian Exposition was held in Chicago in 1893.

It was time to celebrate the 400th anniversary of Christopher Columbus's landing in America. Many cities wanted to host the fair, but Chicago won the competition. Chicago politicians bragged so much about their own city that one newspaper editor in New York City called them "windy politicians." Soon Chicago became known as the "Windy City."

During the next three years, people turned a 630-acre swamp into a "city" of statues, fountains, and buildings where the fair would take place. A group of architects designed the buildings. Sophia Hayden was one of the first women to ever graduate from college with a degree in architecture. She designed a building named the Woman's Building that celebrated all the great things that women did.

The exposition opened May 1, 1893. During its six-month run, over 27 million visitors enjoyed the exhibits. The exposition celebrated Columbus's landing and showed the **determination** and energy of Chicago.

Chicago during World War I

After the exposition, the United States—and Chicago—had a lot to celebrate. But in 1914, World War I raged across Europe. When the United States entered the war in 1917, Chicago played a part. Chicago's Municipal Pier No. 2 opened in 1916 as a place for both business and fun. During the war years, the Red Cross was on the pier. Other groups involved in the war were based on the pier, too.

World War I did not stop **industry** in Chicago. In 1918, for example, two men started making radio equipment on their kitchen tables. Only a year later, they had a large company, the Zenith Radio Corporation. Companies like the Auto-Electric Company were already a big part of Chicago's business community. As early as 1904, that company was building a tunnel system to wire 20,000 telephones in Chicago.

Look for Yourself

Navy Pier
Today, Municipal Pier No. 2 is called Navy Pier. Navy Pier attracts tourists from around the world to its children's museum, boat tours of Chicago, and many other activities.

Municipal Pier No. 2 opened in 1916.

Navy Pier is popular with tourists today.

The Palace of Fine Arts, built for the Columbian Exposition, is now home to the Museum of Science and Industry.

During the Depression, many Chicagoans lost their jobs.
They had to stand in lines like this one to get free food.

The Depression and recovery

In the early twentieth century, the population of Chicago continued to grow. Thousands of African Americans came from the South looking for jobs and freedom from **prejudice.** In 1920, 44,000 African Americans lived in Chicago. By 1930, that number had climbed to more than 230,000. Many people found jobs in steel mills, packing plants, and people's homes. However, it would not always be easy for them to keep working.

In 1929, the **Great Depression** started. Many people around the world lost money and jobs. Many people in Chicago lost their jobs, and African Americans who had just moved to Chicago suffered, too. Instead of giving up hope, many people in Chicago, including African Americans, became involved in the city government and ran for offices in the state government. The community became stronger than it was before.

Franklin D. Roosevelt became president of the United States in 1932. His biggest goal was to end the Depression. With new ideas, President Roosevelt helped the United States slowly recover. While he was president, the Depression ended and the United States became involved in World War II. After World War II, the soldiers came home and started working again, so businesses grew. Chicago became even larger than it was before.

Chicago—and the suburbs—continue to grow

The population of the city continued to grow until 1950, when the city had its highest population. That year, 3.6 million people lived in Chicago. The population was also spreading out from Chicago. The suburbs, smaller towns that were built on the edges of Chicago, were becoming popular places to live. When new expressways were built, people who lived in the suburbs could reach downtown Chicago even faster.

In the 1960s, new expressways made getting to downtown Chicago faster and easier.

Chicago People

Ludwig Mies van der Rohe
In the 1950s, many famous architects helped develop new buildings in Chicago. Mies van der Rohe designed twenty buildings for what is now the Illinois Institute of Technology. The street in front of Chicago's Museum of Contemporary Art is named in honor of Mies van der Rohe.

Mies van der Rohe designed these apartment buildings on Lake Shore Drive.

Chapter 5

Chicago Today

The neighborhoods in Chicago today show the rich history of the city. The neighborhoods also show the changes in the groups of people that come to live there.

A city of neighborhoods

Today, there are still many different cultural groups living in Chicago. The South Side of Chicago is still the heart of the African-American community. The DuSable Museum of African-American History helps the community celebrate successes of African Americans in Chicago. Chicago also has a thriving Chinatown. The Pilsen area, which was once home to large Polish and Czech communities, is now an area where many Latinos live. Many Polish people still live in Chicago. In fact, Chicago has more Polish people than any other city outside of Warsaw, Poland. You can learn more by visiting the Polish Museum of America in Wicker Park. Each of Chicago's many cultural groups helps make this city a great and exciting place to be.

Each neighborhood is special. For example, the Northwest Side has bungalows like these and the West Side has murals showing images of Mexican art.

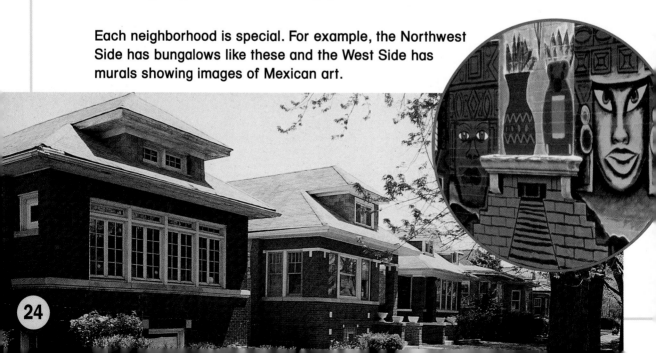

Chicago government

Today, Chicago is run by the mayor and the 50 elected aldermen and alderwomen. The aldermen and alderwomen represent the different neighborhoods and are part of the City Council. The City Council passes laws and makes decisions that help the city government work.

Chicago People

Harold Washington

Harold Washington was born in Chicago. He served as a lawyer and an Illinois state representative. In 1983, Harold Washington was the first African American to be elected mayor of Chicago. He was reelected in 1987, but died of a heart attack later that year.

Chicago helps its people

The city government provides many different services. Chicago provides police and fire protection. The city provides places to stay during severe freezes and heat waves. Snow is removed in the winter, and garbage is picked up year-round. Health centers and city parks are just a few of the many other services that the city government offers. As one of the United States' largest cities, Chicago's government takes care of almost three million people every day.

What does Chicago look like today?

People living in Chicago today enjoy one of the most interesting cities in the world. People here enjoy sports, music, stage shows, and museums. The businesses in Chicago range from the historic meatpacking industry to high-tech computer companies. Visitors from all over come to the city to enjoy Chicago's sights and sounds. Chicago has a remarkable history, and the city continues to grow and thrive.

There are nearly 14,000 police officers in the city of Chicago.

Landmarks

The Art Institute

The Art Institute of Chicago was constructed for the World's Columbian Exposition and became the Art Institute in 1893. The Institute houses a museum as well as an art school.

O'Hare Airport

O'Hare Airport is one of the world's largest and busiest airports. Flights travel between O'Hare and places all around the world.

Tribune Tower

The *Chicago Tribune* had a contest for "the most beautiful office building in the world" in 1922. This building houses the newspaper and includes 120 stones from landmarks around the world.

Wrigley Field

The Chicago Cubs have played baseball at Wrigley Field since 1916. Most scoreboards use machines to change numbers, but Wrigley's scoreboard is changed by people. The scoreboard has never been hit by a batted ball.

University of Chicago

The University of Chicago was founded by John D. Rockefeller. The chapel is one of the most historic buildings at the school.

The Sears Tower

For many years, the Sears Tower was the tallest building in the world. It soars 110 stories high.

Chicago Timeline

1803 Fort Dearborn is built near Lake Michigan.

1673 Father Jacques Marquette and Louis Joliet travel through the Chicago area.

1779 Jean Baptiste Pointe du Sable builds the first settler home.

1865 The Union Stock Yard opens on Christmas Day.

1837 Chicago becomes a city.

1600   1700   1800

Robie House

The famous architect Frank Lloyd Wright built a home for bicycle manufacturer Frederick C. Robie. The style of the building reminded people of the flat land in the Midwest.

Hull House

Jane Addams and Ellen Gates Starr opened Hull House as a settlement house in 1889 to take care of poor people in Chicago. The original dining hall and Hull mansion were preserved, and are still standing today!

Lincoln Park Zoo

One of the country's few major zoos with free admission, the Lincoln Park Zoo has been around for over 100 years. Over three million visitors enjoy the zoo each year.

Carson Pirie Scott Building

In 1899, architect Louis H. Sullivan built one of the first modern buildings on State Street, the Carson Pirie Scott Building. The first two stories of the building are decorated with sculptures made from iron.

Union Stock Yard Gate

The Union Stock Yard in Chicago closed in 1971, but the entrance to the stockyards still stands. It reminds visitors of the history of Chicago's railroad and livestock businesses.

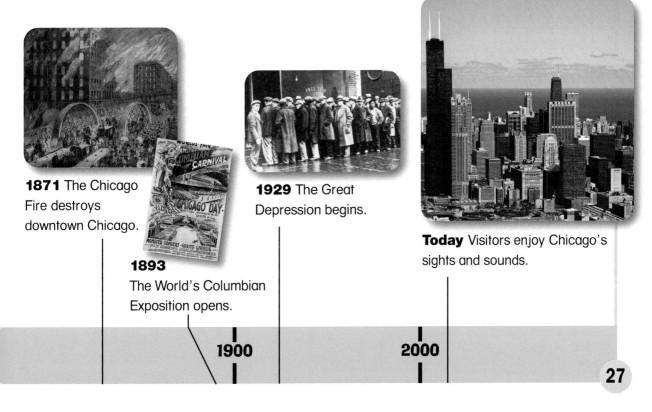

1871 The Chicago Fire destroys downtown Chicago.

1893 The World's Columbian Exposition opens.

1929 The Great Depression begins.

Today Visitors enjoy Chicago's sights and sounds.

1900

2000

Chicago People

Jane Addams (1860-1935)

Jane Addams and her friend Ellen Starr set up a home in a poor neighborhood in Chicago. The home provided shelter, medicine, education, and child care to the people who came there.

Jane Addams

Ida B. Wells Barnett (1862-1931)

Ida Wells was a teacher and writer who fought for the rights of African Americans. She helped start groups that would work for creating equal rights for all people.

Daniel Burnham (1846-1912)

An architect, Daniel Burnham was responsible for some of Chicago's most important buildings. As a city planner, he supervised the World's Columbian Exposition and the planning of the city of Chicago.

Richard J. Daley (1902-1976)

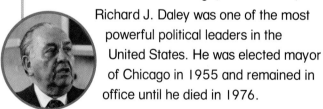

Richard J. Daley was one of the most powerful political leaders in the United States. He was elected mayor of Chicago in 1955 and remained in office until he died in 1976.

Richard J. Daley

Jean Baptiste Pointe du Sable (1745-1818)

Jean Baptiste Pointe du Sable was the first pioneer to build a home on the frontier that would become Chicago. He was a farmer from Haiti who married a Potawatomi woman.

Marshall Field (1834-1906)

Marshall Field owned a store in the city and became the wealthiest Chicagoan of his era. He donated money to found the Field Museum of Natural History.

José Gonzales (1933-)

Chicago is famous for its beautiful murals throughout town. José Gonzales is a muralist and founder of the Chicano art movement in Chicago.

Jesse Jackson (1941-)

Jesse Jackson worked with Martin Luther King Jr. to help fight racial prejudice in the United States. Jackson formed Operation PUSH (People United to Serve Humanity) and the National Rainbow Coalition.

Jesse Jackson

Helmut Jahn (1940-)

Helmut Jahn is a German-born architect who designed the modern State of Illinois Center, now the James R. Thompson Center. He teaches architecture at many major universities in the United States.

Louis Joliet (1645-1700)

Along with Jacques Marquette, Louis Joliet explored much of the Mississippi River and Illinois and Wisconsin. Joliet was a French-Canadian who was well-trained in making maps of waterways.

Jacques Marquette (1637-1675)

Jacques Marquette was a French explorer who traveled with Louis Joliet. The two men discovered water routes between the Great Lakes and the Mississippi River.

Edward "Butch" O'Hare (1914-1943)

Fighter pilot Butch O'Hare was a hero who was killed during World War II. The City of Chicago named the city's major airport in his honor.

Bill Pinkney (1935-)

Born in Chicago, Bill Pinkney was the first African American to sail around the world alone. He is captain of a ship that is an exact copy of the slave ship *Amistad.* He teaches people about the importance of equality for all people.

Louis H. Sullivan (1856-1924)

Louis H. Sullivan was an architect who created beautiful Chicago skyscrapers. He designed the Auditorium Building for Roosevelt University and the Carson Pirie Scott building.

Frank Lloyd Wright (1867-1959)

Architect Frank Lloyd Wright started his career in Chicago by designing Prairie Style homes. He designed the Guggenheim Museum in New York City and was one of the country's most important architects.

Chicago Mayors and Years in Office

First Mayor:
William Butler Ogden 1837–1838

Carter Henry Harrison Jr. 1897–1905, 1911–1915

Edward Fitzsimmons Dunne 1905–1907

Fred A. Busse 1907–1911

William Hale Thompson 1915–1923, 1927–1931

William Emmett Dever 1923–1927

Anton Joseph Cermak 1931–1933

Frank J. Corr 1933

Edward Joseph Kelly 1933–1947

Martin H. Kennelly 1947–1955

Richard Joseph Daley 1955–1976

Michael Anthony Bilandic 1976–1979

Jane Margaret Byrne 1979–1983

Harold Washington 1983–1987

David Duvall Orr 1987

Eugene Sawyer 1987–1989

Richard Michael Daley 1989–present

There have been a total of 45 mayors of Chicago. Before 1907, mayors served two-year terms. Beginning in 1907, mayors served four-year terms. The first primary election for mayor was held in February 1911.

Chicago Maps and Almanac

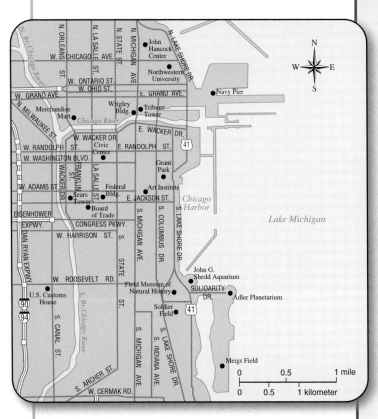

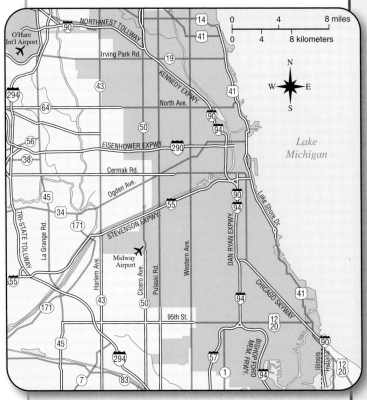

World's largest ...

Commercial office building:
Merchandise Mart

Free public zoo:
Lincoln Park Zoo

Food festival:
Taste of Chicago

Busiest roadway:
Dan Ryan Expressway

Chicago, home of the first ...

Steel-framed skyscraper, 1885

Elevated railway, 1892

Zipper, 1896

All-Star baseball game, 1933

Car race, 1895

Chicago has ...

30,000,000 visitors annually

2,890,000 residents

13,550 police officers

7,000+ restaurants

4,260 firefighters

3,780 miles of streets

560 parks

491 public elementary schools

200 live theaters

92 public high schools

64 miles of expressway

49 museums

46 movable bridges

31 miles of lakefront

7 public colleges

4 public universities

Glossary

American Revolution *(also called the Revolutionary War)* war fought by the American colonies from 1775 to 1783 to gain their independence from England

canal waterway dug across land for ships or small boats to go through or to carry water to places that need it

Civil War war between the Northern and Southern states of the United States from 1861 to 1865

compete to try hard to win or gain something wanted by others

determination great purpose in carrying out an activity

fertile producing crops easily

Great Depression time when business activity was slow and many people were out of work. The Great Depression in the United States started in 1929.

immigrant person who comes into a foreign country or region to live

Industrial Revolution widespread replacement of manual labor by machines, which began in Great Britain in the eighteenth century and is still continuing in some parts of the world

industry any form of business, manufacture, or trade

merchant person who runs a business

prejudice opinion formed without taking time and care to judge fairly

sewage waste matter that passes through sewers, or underground drains

sprawl to spread out in an irregular way

tragedy very sad or terrible happening

More Books to Read

Aylesworth, Thomas, and Virginia Aylesworth. *Chicago.* Farmington Hills, Mich.: Blackbirch Press, 1990.

Basye, Ann. *Kids in the Loop: Chicago Adventures for Kids and Their Grown-Ups.* Chicago: Chicago Review Press, 1995.

Doherty, Craig A., and Katherine M. Doherty. *The Sears Tower.* Farmington Hills, Mich.: Blackbirch Press, 1995.

McNulty, Elizabeth. *Chicago Then and Now.* Holt, Mich.: Thunder Bay Press, 2000.

Stein, Conrad R. *Chicago.* Danbury, Conn.: Children's Press, 1997.

Chicago Motto:

Urbs in horto, which is Latin for "city in a garden."

Index